DIVINE BLESSINGS

JOYCE WILLIAMS GRAVES

†

Are Gifts from a Sovereign God

Believe in God the Father, Jesus, Son of God, and the Holy Spirit.

Joyce Williams Graves

Wait on the Lord be of good courage, and He shall strengthen thine heart: wait, I say, on the Lord. Psalm 27:14 **kjv**

Jesus saith unto Him, I am the way, the truth, and the life: no man cometh unto the Father, but by me. John 14:6 **kjv**

Rejoice in the Lord always: and again, I say, Rejoice.

Let your moderation be known unto all men. The Lord is at hand.

Be careful for nothing; but in everything by prayer and supplication with thanksgiving let your requests be made known unto God. Philippians 4:4-8 **kjv**

*****

Start each day with a grateful heart :-)

DIVINE

BLESSINGS

JOYCE WILLIAMS GRAVES

Are Gifts from a Sovereign God

508 West 26th Street KEARNEY, NE 68848
402-819-3224
info@medialiteraryexcellence.com

Thank you for purchasing my book. But who am I and what do I believe?

Who am I?		What do I Believe?

I am a child of God		I believe in the one God I believe in Jesus Christ I believe in Holy Spirit I believe in the Bible

God performs countless miracles and fills our lives with Divine blessing!

*****

"It has been a pleasure getting to know Mrs. Joyce Williams Graves. She is a kind and encouraging woman who supports others. It's a breath of fresh air knowing someone always cheering you on authentically. Joyce is a woman with integrity, courage, and honor. She loves the Lord!"

—Jennifer Foxworthy, Founder and CEO of Inspirationally Speaking, LLC and Unstoppable You Ministries Inc.

I have known Joyce for close to 30 years, she is one of the warmest caring people I have the pleasure to know. Her gentle smile reveals her inner glow which is clearly grounded in her faith.

—Tom McNamara, Retired Vallejo, California

Glen, my husband shared his Divine Blessing with me. He said, having his ninety-one-year-old Mother, Annie Graves, still alive is one of his Divine Blessings. His Mother can eat her food without any assistance and is able to dress by herself. He is divinely blessed to have a church home to attend every Sunday with his wife. He's grateful to be married to his wife for thirteen years. He is still working and has been at his present job for thirty years.

"He is so thankful for his good health at seventy-one years old. God has made a way out of no way for Him. Despite the differences within his family and sometimes his friends, he's very thankful and grateful for God's love for Him, which helps Him to love people even more."

"He is a child of God and a believer of scripture, John 3:16, 'For God so loved the world, that He gave his only begotten Son, that whosoever believeth in Him should not perish, but have everlasting life.' He is divinely blessed for His Savior and his love for Him."

**—Glen Emmanuel Graves, Senior Deacon,
Forest Heights Baptist Church, Fort Washington, Maryland**

"My big sister, spiritual guidance, friend, mother, grandmother, wife, and godmother to others. I have known Joyce for about 34 years, she is a person that Love the Lord and make God first in her life as well as family. Joyce is a person that will go that extra mile or step to help out no matter what she already has on her plate, she is a blessing to be in your life because she will give her true opinion on matters, she listens and will make time for you, I love my sister Joyce for the person she is and only wish there were more people like her. Thank you for being in my life and Godson of Jaylen."

**—Mazie Williams, Mazie's Fragrances,
Charlotte, North Carolina**

I have known Joyce Graves for a few years, and she has helped my family in a business capacity. From my first interaction with Joyce, it was very clear that she was very compassionate about her spiritual beliefs. She has a deep passion for writing and through her writing she so eloquently expresses her spiritual thoughts. She believed her written words could unlock the doors of the reader's imagination.

Harold L. Robinson Sr

Retired Friend

Deaconess Joyce Graves is a member of Forest Heights Baptist Church. (FHBC) As her pastor I must say she is a blessing to FHBC, and especially in support to me as her pastor.

Deaconess Graves in the past three "Covid" years as Chair of our Usher Board, she has made changes that has improved our Sunday service as we moved from our sanctuary to Zoom video.

It is must important for a pastor to have someone to monitor the needs of the pastor during the church service and from that perspective I commend Deaconess Graves for her dedication in support of her pastor.

These few words from my perspective may seem frivolous to some, but the word of God says. "Withhold not good from them to whom it is due, when it is in the power of thine hand to do it," (Proverbs 3:27 KJV)

Joyce I am proud of you, I truly appreciate your dedication, and support of your pastor and guest preachers.

You bring to memory the women who supported Jesus and the 12 disciples as He minister to the people in Galilee – Jerusalem. (Luke 8:1-3 KJV)

—Blessings
Reverend William Jones, Sr.
Pastor, Forest Heights Baptist Church
Oxon Hill, Maryland.

I believe God uses others to help us when its needed and Joyce has been there to help me personally, she also assists with the business of the church, and aid her community, all done with infectious smile.

For me she is a friend, a prayer partner, and a supporter. During the day I receive texts from her that lift my spirits with messages of love, strength, and encouragement. The times I was recovering from sickness she even brought food by.

In the Church, Joyce can be seen in many capacities. While she uses her voice and leadership skills to Lead as head of the Usher Board, the Libarian, and the Historian. She also assists the finance office, and the Deaconess. And with her knowledge of technology, she has helped establish the FHBC website.

When Joyce is not working with the church, she is out supporting the community lending a hand with food delivery, clothing and even giving bible to those who might not be able obtain them.

Finally, in all she does for others, the church and community, we are all consumed with that infectious smile especially when she shares her love for her Lord and Savior.

—Mrs. Jerri Jones – First Lady
Forest Heights Baptist Church
Prince George County
Oxon Hill, Maryland

Praise the Lord

Blessed is those who fear the Lord,
who find great delight in His commands. Their children will be
mighty in the land; the generation of the upright will be blessed.
Wealth and riches are in their houses,
and their righteousness endures forever.
Even in darkness light dawns for the upright,

for those who are gracious and compassionate and righteous. Good
will come to those who are generous and lend freely, who conduct
their affairs with justice.

Surely the righteous will never be shaken;
They will be remembered forever.
They will have no fear of bad news.

Their hearts are steadfast, trusting in the Lord. Their hearts are
secure; they will have no fear; In the end they will look in triumph on
their foes. They have freely scattered their gifts to the poor; their
righteousness endures forever. their horn will be lifted high in honor.

The intent of this book is to give hope, faith, optimism, motivation, encouragement, joy, and inspiration for you to live your life, like tomorrow may not come. Yes, one day we will leave this world. But, while you are here, get your diving blessings.

I want everyone to know whether you believe in my God, Jesus Christ, the Holy Spirit is real or not, know this, HE LOVES YOU! The Holy Bible says He does. I believe in Him, and you should also believe Him. We live here on earth, who is the Creator of this planet, not man! No. It's what is said in the book of Gensis, in the beginning God created the heavens and the earth. The Bible has been around for millions of years, maybe more. It is completely true and applicable today. If you can believe in the air you breathe, you can believe in the Holy Bible.

Brothers and sisters, please believe that our God is all about Love. I hope the many words in my book will bring peace, tranquility, and harmony into your life. May my words be a reminder of God's love, guidance, and his many Divine blessings for all of us. My brothers and sisters, He loves you, and so do I.

Praise God from whom all blessing flows.

*****

If you can read these seven words, then you have been blessed by someone who taught you how to read!

Remember, things we take for granted, someone else is praying for.

———

You want your Divine Blessing

But seek ye first kingdom of God, and his righteousness; and all these things shall be added unto you. Matthew 6:33

CONTENTS

PREFACE

Being a Blessing

Being a Divine Blessing is not just a privilege to do occasionally each day. No, it's an honor to show charity and compassion in a very thoughtful and kind way.

Take time to seek ways to be caring and considerate. You see it's not very hard, especially when you ask God to help you; just be still, listen for His whisper, and don't discard.

Always keep your head up, for blessings fall from above. May your blessings outnumber the flowers that grow? and the Lord will be with you wherever you go.

Remember, in every storm there's a blessing. And, in every blessing a quiet storm is removed.

May the blessings you give, always return to you.

Divine Blessing from God's Promises
Claim them over you

Our Lord and Savior has given many promises to us. Let me share a few divine blessings found in the Holy Bible.

"Have I not commanded you? Be strong and courageous. Do not be afraid; do not be discouraged, for the Lord your God will be with you wherever you go."

"Do not fear [anything], for I am with you; Do not be afraid, for I am your God. I will strengthen you, be assured I will help you; I will certainly take hold of you with My righteous right hand [a hand of justice, of power, of victory, of salvation."

"If you remain in me, and my words remain in you, you will ask whatever you desire, and it will be done for you. |John 15:7"

"Thou wilt keep Him in perfect peace, whose mind is stayed on thee: because He trusteth in thee."

"The LORD your God is among you; He is mighty to save. He will rejoice over you with gladness; He will quiet you with His love; He will rejoice over you with singing."

Meet Joyce Williams Graves

You must meet Joyce Williams Graves. Ask her how she's doing, and you will hear these words, "I am blessed." Blessed is one of her favorite words. She is a true child of God. She loves the Lord and all He has done for her in her life. She is not ashamed of the Gospel of Christ. Joyce has lived her life, so far, with all vigor, energy, and passion. She awakes every morning to try to be a blessing to anyone she can.

God has blessed her to become a daughter, wife, mother, grandmother, great grandmother, sister, and loyal friend. She's a writer, an author, poet, playwright, numismatist, artist, sculptor, US notary public, and business owner. She loves biblical and ancient history.

This poetry collection delves deep into Joyce's values and beliefs that were learned from her parents and from meditating on God's Holy Word. She hopes that you will enjoy these spirit-filled and heartfelt poems about her life and life's day-to-day pleasures, trials, and tribulations. Her ultimate prayer is that everyone will know that we all serve a sovereign Lord who loves each one of us unconditionally and endlessly. You have so much to gain when you know Him and everything to lose if you choose otherwise.

Look to the Lord and His strength; seek his face always. (Psalm 105:4)

Thankful, grateful, and blessed is exactly how I feel about you for purchasing my poetry book. Well, maybe you are just reviewing it, and that's okay also. I would like to acknowledge how thankful I am that you have considered peeking at this collection of my work. I'm deeply grateful for an audience who supports others—me.

I am truly appreciative to God for bringing you into a small part of my world through this book.

Joyce hope and prayer in writing this book is that more and more people would meditate with me on God's Holy Word and be grateful for all his many blessings in our lives.

I have asked God to please give me whatever I need to bless someone every single day. God blesses us when we bless, help, and pray for others.

I pray with all my heart this collage of my writings will inspire you, lift your spirits, and make you smile. Also, I pray that my words will help you find a more intimate relationship with God.

I thank God for the good and bad experiences in my life, for they have shaped my spiritual and secular life, my mind, and my writings.

ACKNOWLEDGEMENT

Father God, this book is dedicated to you. I am extremely grateful to you and your Son, Jesus Christ, for your love for me. There are not enough words to express my sincere love for you and all the beautiful things you have done for me, my family, and friends. My life has been divinely blessed with your sincere love for me. This endeavor would not have been possible without your love as a father for me. My earthly father is gone now; however, you have replaced Him in my life. I could not have undertaken this journey without you and your Son, Jesus Christ.

You listen to me when I cry out in my pain and sorrow and let me know you are always there for me with my questions, issues, and concerns. Your steadfast love never ceases. Your mercies never come to an end; they are new every morning. Great is your faithfulness, Father.

Father, I am an incomplete soul, yet you still love me completely. Even though I am imperfect, you love me perfectly. Many days I felt lost, though I may feel lost and without compass, Father, your love encompasses me completely. You love all of us, even those who are rejected, flawed, awkward, sorrowful, or broken. We love you back, Father.

Your love is shown in my many divine blessings, daily. You show your love in the beauty of creation, the friends you have given me, and the people you placed in my life.

Father, thank you from the bottom of my heart. Thank you for sending your Son, Jesus Christ into my life.

INTRODUCTION

Joyce Williams Graves is a poetess who has written the unspoken word for many years and now shares her words of expressions, and the innermost emotions of her heart with others. Joyce writes short stories, prose, free verse, and style, rhythmic, spiritual, acrostic, haiku, and senryu forms of poetry. Her select poems of emotions and expressions are on love, giving, serving, values, passion, spiritual, friendship, family, life, inspiration, nature, and humor. Joyce hopes that her poems will give encouragement to the discouraged, joy and hope to the sorrowful, inspiration to the hopeless, happiness, and a warm smile to the brokenhearted. She has learned over time, when life's pitfalls are deeply rooted, burdens are many, and sufferings seem to steadily increase in her life. That's when she places her trust in God. He is always faithful with his unconditional love for her. Yes, her God is enough!

Joyce is a playwright producing her first play, *Cotton Field to Concert Hall*, cowritten with playwright, Ellen Wiggins in March 2017.

In addition, Joyce is working on her third inspirational and spiritual book tentatively called "Divine Blessings". Her first fictional and spiritual book, *Jesus, I Don't Understand*, was published in May 2014. *"Be A Blessing to Someone today, for Tomorrow May Be Your Blessing."* is Joyce's second spiritual book.

Jesus, I Don't Understand.
Be a Blessing to Someone Today, For Tomorrow May Be Your Blessing.

A Smile

is a nice accompaniment to your attire.
It gives others a wonderful reason to smile back at you.
Is remembered longer than a frown.
is a friendly way to greet people.
hides the pain of a broken soul.
shows others you have not given up on life. Is

Why not be a blessing to everyone you
meet with a genuine honest smile?
a great way to start your day, any day!
promotes encouragement, confidence, and hope.
Is a special gift to a stranger to stranger?
If you know God, you will always have a reason to smile.

"If you only have one smile in you, give it to the people you love."
(Maya Angelou)

Dedication

My book, "Divine Blessings" is dedicated to my Lord and Savior, my God, the Creator of the whole world, Jesus Christ, his only begotten son, the King of Kings, Lord of lords, and our Father in Heaven. I love His precious son; Jesus Christ for He has blessed me in so many special ways every day of my life. When I woke up this morning, it was because of my God, Lord and Savior's mercy and grace in my life. Brothers and Sisters serve God with your whole heart, for He loves you. You can never go wrong serving God.

He also blesses my family, friends and even strangers with his love. Because of God, Jesus's Father said, "all things are possible" through His son Jesus Christ. Jesus looked at them and said, "With man this is impossible, but with God all things are possible." Matthew 19:26. I was able write this book with my faith and my love for God, Jesus and the Holy Spirt because God loves me and wants the best for me. I love you God, Lord of my life. I will serve you ALWAYS my Father, God, Jesus, His son, and the Holy Spirit, forever because He sacrificed His life for me and the whole world. All we need to do is love and serve Him with our whole heart, soul, strength, and mind. Thank you so much, God for loving me, my family, and others.

My Christian Faith – My Life & Autobiography

I am humbly grateful for the unconditional love from my Savior, Father God, His Son, Jesus Christ, the King of Kings, and the Holy Spirit. I am the daughter of Philip Daniel and Catherine Mae Samuels; both are deceased (2000 & 2015). I am their fourth child and have four siblings (three sisters, Jackie, Phyllis, and Wanda) and one brother (Connie Cornelius -deceased). I have been married to my husband, Glen Emmanuel Graves for fourteen years, and have a fourteen-year-old black curly hair poodle. I have one son, Monty Eli Williams, a daughter-in-law, Lisa Keith Willians and six grandchildren: Lael Joy, Faith Elaine, Janna Joli, Elijah Strong, Cayden, and Micah Andrew Williams, and my great grandson, Asa Noel. Thank you, Lord, for these beautiful Divine Blessings from you.

My Christian faith is built on God, the Father, the son, Jesus Christ, and the Holy Spirit. I have been a member of Forest Heights Baptist Church (FHBC) in Prince George's Country for over fourteen years. Joyce serves as FHBC Head Usher, Assistance Treasurer, Webmaster, Historian, Librarian and Children's Sunday School Teacher.

Joyce has written two books, "Jesus I Don't Understand', in year 2014 and "Be a Blessing to Someone Today, For Tomorrow May Be Your Blessing, in year 2018." This is her 3rd Christian book.

Joyce has a Bachelor of Science degree in Computer Management and an Advance Master's degree, in Information Technology, with Honors of Distinction. Joyce has many interests and hobbies, such as a Bible Project Ministry, Senior Citizen Love Ministry, Poetry, Painting and Drawing, Piano, Collector of Coins (Numismatics), International and Domestic Traveler, Reading Biblical and Black History, Swimming,

Dominos, and Walking. She is an entrepreneur with a beauty consultant business, Jafra International. Joyce is a playwright. She co-wrote a play called "Cotton Field to Concert Hall." This is a musical journey of a slave girl who transforms herself into her great-great-great-granddaughter and an opera diva, in this multi-genre concert extravaganza. It was performed in 2017 at the Public Playhouse in Lanham, Maryland and in 2018 at the Kennedy Center for the Performing Arts in Washington, DC.

Joyce's love for God is inherently in her DNA. She prays for her family, friends, neighbors and even strangers, regularly. God loves all of us.

Please pray for the world, Israel, and Zion!

Some *of My Divine Blessings Stories*

I have been given many Divine Blessings from the Lord over my lifetime. One Sunday on May 4, 2023, my husband and I were laying in the bed watching a Biblical movie, "the Ten Commandments." But something just didn't feel right to me. I realized I didn't see my dog, Energy. I said, "Glen, where is Energy?" He looked at me with a look of surprise and said, "I don't know, Joyce." Energy is a black fourteen-year-old curly hair poodle, my precious baby. I bought Energy when He was 8 weeks on a side street in Washington, in March 2009. Anyway, I got up to look for Him and Glen followed me throughout our home. We looked all over our home for five minutes. My God! Energy was not anywhere to be found. So out of the back door in a panic we rushed outback to look for my baby. Around back calling his name, "Energy!" but He was nowhere to be found. Tears flowing down my eyes, I knew He must have gotten out of the backyard gate. Oh No! I got dressed and found my hat, (It was raining a little outside) and put it on my bad hair day. We jumped in the truck in front of the garage and hurried to find my baby. We went down the street and got to the end of it and Glen asked, "which way should we go". I wasn't sure, but told Him, "Let's go to the left." As I looked down the street to my left, I saw two ladies, and a little girl standing on the corner, and it looked like my Energy was there with them.

Once the traffic was clear hubby made a left turn and pulled right beside the threesome. My heart was beating a mile a minute, not 10 miles a minute. Out of our truck I ran towards my dog looking at the ladies with a HUGE smile on my face and thankfulness in my heart. I was so grateful because Energy had to cross a busy street to get to that side of the street. That was my first 'Divine Blessing that day." Energy is alive and back in my arms once again. I was so happy. We thanked the two angels and prayed with them. I turned towards Glen to give Him Energy to put in the truck. Before I knew it, I had stepped off the curb without looking, and fell straight backwards to the street and hit my head on the sidewalk. It happened so fast! One minute, I was standing with my precious baby in my arms, then the next minute my head was on the payment sidewalk curb. My second Divine Blessing! Praise God, I landed on the back of my head and not my face~ Praise God. Oh yes, it hurt so bad, but my face wasn't messed up. The ladies and Glen helped me up. Of course, Glen wanted to rush me to straight to the nearest hospital. Stubborn me, I didn't go. Two days later my neck on the left side was killing me. Five days later I finally went to my doctor. His analysis was, I had pulled a disc in my neck. He said, "Joyce you will be fine over time, my 3rd Divine Blessing!"

I should have gone to my physician doctor when I fell and hit my head. Stubborn Me! I am very sorry I didn't get the ladies home address, so I could send them a "Thank you card" for holding Energy until we were able to get Him back. I believe God knew my love for my dog and blessed me to place those these ladies at the right place and time for me to get Energy back. When God blesses you, always take a moment, to say, "Thank you, Lord. My neck is fine today, many months later."

Love – Faith – Obedience

Love is something you do!

Only what you do for Christ will last.

Without Faith it's impossible to please God.

Get outside of your comfort zone and do whatever God wants you to do. Be obedient.

Twenty Ways to Be a Divine Blessing to Someone

No Act of Kindness Is Too Small

- Deliver a meal to someone or a treat to a coworker, friend, or neighbor for lunch.
- Call a neighbor to see if she/he needs anything from the grocery store before you go.
- Send or bring flowers to someone who may need a little pick-me-up.
- Be a mentor to a friend or coworker's son or daughter for a month.
- Send a "Thinking of You" card to someone you know.
- Help a neighbor or friend with a project or chore.
- Invite a neighbor or friend to your home to have a cooked meal.
- Offer to babysit for free for a friend, family member, or coworker.
- Pay for someone's coffee or meal behind you in the drive-through line.
- Send a note or letter of encouragement to a young person,
- Give another driver your parking spot.
- Give a little treat to the postman, policeman, or delivery person. Just put it in your mailbox for Him or her.
- Leave a generous tip for a waiter or waitress.
- Take the time to pray for someone who is in need.
- Invite your neighbor or coworker to your next backyard barbecue.
- Pay for one movie ticket of the person behind you in line.
- Slip $20 to someone who you know is struggling financially. Be discreet.

- Call a senior friend and see if his/her day is going OK.

- Pay for someone's meal or dessert at a restaurant.

- Take two lunches to the next business meeting.

- Bake some goodies and take them to the homeless facility, shelter, police or fire station, or hospital.

- Take a box of donuts to a senior center, a school, or a local office, etc.

- Pray for your church, neighborhood, school, or local business.

- Spend an afternoon helping at a homeless shelter.

- Take two cups of latte to work for your coworker or boss.

"And whatever you do, whether in word or deed, do it all in the name of the Lord Jesus, giving thanks to God the Father through Him." (Colossians 3:17)

Great Divine Blessing Quotes

- If we count our **blessings** instead of our money, we would all be rich.

- Talk about your **blessings** more than you talk about your burdens.

- "Kind words are such a **blessing** to the needy, if one but knew the pleasure that they bring." (John McLeod, my son's basketball coach).

- Get up in the morning knowing that God gave you everything to fulfill your destiny or your day.

- Having somewhere to go is home, having someone to love is family, having both is a **blessing**.

- Don't think of things you didn't get after praying. Think of the countless **blessings** you have received without asking.

- Feel God in every gentle touch. See God in every happy face. Hear God in every caring word. Receive God's **blessings** every day of your life.

- Yesterday is long gone; tomorrow is a mystery; today is a beautiful **blessing**.

- A contented mind is the greatest **blessing** a man can enjoy in the world.

- Forget the day's troubles; remember the day's **blessings**.

- "Never retaliate when people say unkind things about you. Pay them back with a **blessing**, and God will bless you." (1 Peter 3:9)

- God's **blessings** may come as a surprise and how much you receive depends on how much your heart can believe.

*May you be **blessed** beyond what you expect.*

Supreme Blessedness Beatitudes from God

Taken from Matthew 5:3–12

- Bless the poor in spirit: for theirs is the kingdom of heaven.

- Bless is they that mourn for they shall be comforted.

- Bless is the meek: for they shall inherit the earth.

- Bless are they which do hunger and thirst after righteousness: for they shall be filled.

- Bless is the merciful: for they shall obtain mercy.

- Bless is the pure in heart: for they shall see God.

- Bless is the peacemakers: for they shall be called the children of God.

- Bless is they which are persecuted for righteousness' sake: for theirs is the kingdom of heaven.

- Bless is when men shall revile you, and persecute you, and shall say all manner of evil against you falsely, for my sake.

- Rejoice, and be exceeding glad: for great is your reward in heaven: for so persecuted they the prophets which were before you.

The word *beatitude* comes from the Latin *beatitudo*, meaning **"blessedness."**

Ordinary men and women
who was Divinely Blessed by God

In the Holy Bible years ago and even today, God has divinely blessed many ordinary men and women in the world, like you and me.

Therefore, the promise comes by faith, so that it may be by grace and may be guaranteed to all Abraham's offspring—not only to those who are of the law but also to those who have the faith of Abraham. He is the father of us all. As it is written: "I have made you a father of many nations." He is our father in the sight of God, in whom He believed— the God who gives life to the dead and calls into being things that we're not.

Against all hope, Abraham in hope believed and so became the father of many nations, just as it had been said to Him, "So shall your offspring be." Without weakening in his faith, He faced the fact that his body was as good as dead—since He was about a hundred years old—and that Sarah's womb was also dead. Yet He did not waver through unbelief regarding the promise of God but was strengthened in his faith and gave glory to God, being fully persuaded that God had power to do what he had promised. This is why "it was credited to Him as righteousness." Romans 4:16-22

My heavenly father is God, my earthly fathers
are Abraham, and Philip Daniel Samuels.

<u>Abraham, an ordinary faithful man</u> was divinely blessed by God. He promised, Abraham and his barren wife, Sarah that she will have a son by her husband, and Abraham will become the Father of many nations. To this day, in the year 2023. Abraham is still considered the father of the many nations. God gave Abraham and Sarah a son named Isaac. God also blessed Abraham and Sarah with many other children. In our world today, there are many women who will never have children, God does what pleases Him. But God blessed these two persons richly with a son. His name was Isaac. Also, He even gave Isaac two of his own sons, Esau, and Jacob. Also, God divinely blessed Abraham's sons.

Rahab, an ordinary Hebrew woman received a Divine Blessing from the God. She was a Canaanite woman living in Jericho, Rahab was also a prostitute who was also a biblical heroine. Rahab was according to the Book of Joshua, a woman who lived in Jericho in the Promised Land and assisted the Israelites in capturing the city by hiding two men who had been sent to scout the city prior to their attack. God said only Rahab the prostitute shall live, she and all who are with her in the house, because she hid the messengers that they sent. God's Divine Blessing redeemed Rahab from prostitution to become the ancestress not only of David the king but of Jesus the Messiah (Ruth 4:18-22; Matt 1:3-16). God's ability to redeem our past and grace our future exceeds our imagination.

Rahab agreed to help the spies, so she hid them on her roof. The king's men searched Rahab's house but could not find the spies. After they left, Rahab asked the spies to protect her family when their army came to fight against Jericho. The spies promised Rahab that her family would be safe. And they were protected! Another Divine Blessing!

Noah of the Old Testament was Divinely Blessed by the Lord. Noah was a righteous man and the grandson of Methuselah, the oldest person in the Bible, who died at 969 years old in the year of the flood. That's longevity and a divine blessing. He was the tenth generation of Adam, the first human being on earth. Noah's father was Enoch, of whom it is said He "walked with God" (Genesis 5:24), but who was taken to heaven without dying at 365 years. Again, what is a Divine Blessing?

God asked Noah to build an Ark because He was going to destroy the earth with water. Why? His people were corrupt and sinning and did wickedness throughout the world. Noah said He would do what God asked? He was obedient to God's Word. It took 120 years before the flood came, and it did come! God spared Noah's life, his wife, three sons and their son's wives. What divine blessing was given to Noah? Yes, Noah was obedient to God's request of Him, and He was divinely blessed richly by God.

Job, the prophet of the Old Testament was divinely blessed. Most of us know the story of Job. He was an ordinary man. The Bible says He was a righteous and godly man. He was a very wealthy family man with many servants and ten children. What a beautiful blessing? God gave Job a Divine Blessing by protecting Him against the wickedness of Satan, the evil one. Job feared God and was a respectable man. There were many things done to Job's life, especially physically and mentally. Job lost much, his home, livestock and all his children. Yet, Job never turned his feeling or heart against God. He stayed steadfast in his love for the Father. "Satan" was granted permission by the God to test Job's faith and faithfulness. Job's wife and friends turned against Him when Satan did many evil things against Him. But Job stood steadfast for his love for God. And, God gave Job divine blessings, and gave Him double what He loss.

Glen, my husband a humble man shared some of his "Divine Blessings" with me. He said, "Having his ninety-three-year-old Mother, Annie Graves still alive is one of his Divine Blessings." His Mother can eat her food without any assistance and able to get dress by herself. Glen is divinely blessed to have a church home to attend every Sunday with his wife. He's very grateful to be married to his wife for thirteen years. He is still working and has been at his present job for almost thirty years. She's been retired for eleven years and loving it, and love serving her Lord and Savior.

Glen is so thankful for his good health at seventy-two years old this year. God has always made a way out no way for Him. Despite some of the differences within his family and sometimes his friends, He's very thankful and grateful for God's love for Him, which helps Him to love people even more.

Glen is a child of God and a believer of this scripture, John 3:16, "For God so loved the world, that He gave his only begotten Son, that whosoever believeth in Him should not perish, but have everlasting life." He has been divinely blessed from our Savior and God's love for Him. Glen is a good person. I know**, I'm his wife**.

Mary (the virgin Mary) was a first-century Jewish woman of Nazareth, the wife of Joseph and the mother of Christ Jesus. She is described in the Holy Bible as a young virgin who was chosen by Yahweh (God) to conceive Jesus through the Holy Spirit. After giving birth to Jesus in Bethlehem, she raised Him in the city of Nazareth in

Galilee and was in Jerusalem at the time of his crucifixion and with the apostles after his ascension. Because God chose her (her Divine Blessing) to be the mother of His son Jesus Christ. She accepted God's invitation to be the mother of our Savior, Jesus Christ. Her faith and trust in God are a great example to us. To prepare her for this role, by the grace of God, Jesus was born without sin. What is a Divine Blessing?

Think on These Things

God is the source of your Divine Blessings.
You Should Count Your Blessings Daily
You are designed to Smile, not Frown.
Always be kinder than you feel.
People who are faithful are fruitful.
The only thing that limits us is our Faith.
Stand with God and you will never be embarrassed or regret it.

God is my measuring stick.
God is good.
God is the only judge.
Seek God's will always.
God is everywhere!
Always, think about these things daily.

Divine Blessing from God's Promises
Claim them over you!

Our Lord and Savior has given many promises to us. Let me share a few divine blessings found in the Holy Bible.

"Have I not commanded you? Be strong and courageous. Do not be afraid; do not be discouraged, for the Lord your God will be with you wherever you go."

'Do not fear [anything], for I am with you; Do not be afraid, for I am your God. I will strengthen you, be assured I will help you; I will certainly take hold of you with my righteous right hand, a hand of justice, of power, of victory, of salvation.

If you remain in me, and my words remain in you, you will ask whatever you desire, and it will be done for you. | John 15:7

Thou wilt keep Him in perfect peace, whose mind is stayed on thee: because He trusteth in thee.

The LORD your God is among you; He is mighty to save. He will rejoice over you with gladness; He will quiet you with His love; He will rejoice over you with singing."

Seek God Promises

Spiritual
Inspiration
Hope

Create in me a clean heart, O God; and renew a right spirit within me.
Cast me not away from thy presence; and take not thy holy spirit
from me. Restore unto me the joy of thy salvation; and uphold me
with thy free spirit.

(Psalm 51:10)

The Lethal Tongue

Brothers and Sisters use words without any
forethought or consideration to others that can impact
feelings, reactions, and smothers.

Sometimes words hurt more than we will ever know.
Are you careful and mindful?
of what you say to others
or do you just let your words flow?

Yes, even in our God's house,
you should choose your words carefully!
We shouldn't say cruel words, whenever,
wherever, and to whomever.

It's just not right and there's no victory in them!
Words are usually said to be understood, correct?
Are you looking for an opinion,
viewpoint or just to impress?
Meekness in our words
does not mean you are weak;
it's power under control
before one speaks.

Words spoken with wisdom are so
powerful and potent and gives knowledge to
share one's thoughts, feelings, and beliefs. Do we use our words
wisely, when we speak or do we use our lethal tongue
to make your receiver feel weak.

Words of wisdom from above
bring strength and understanding.
A gentle answer turns away wrath.
Harsh words stir up anger.
God is your measuring stick when you speak.

Would he say the words you express? Brothers and sisters, the
tongue is a vessel to help,
encourage, inspire, and motivate the listener. Your
reward in how you use your tongue will be honored and rewarded
by God, the Father and Son.

My Church

Forest Heights Baptist Church

The place to be when troubles call
A timeless space where in hopes dwells
People gather to worship their creator
Heavenly songs, chants and hymns fill the room
Praises and blessings are everywhere,
Faith, Hope, and Love are restored

A fervent place to reclaim what you have lost and maintain what
you gained through the Holy Spirit.

The Greatest Holy man I know.

The Kindest man I know.

The Incarnation of God

The Creator of the World

The Jewish messiah

The Man who is God in the flesh

He is the is the way, the truth, and the life

He is the Prince of Peace.

He walked on Water.

He is the great Physician.

He is our deliver.

He died on the cross for us.

He is our high tower.

He will never leave or forsake us.

Who is He?

He is Our Savior, Christ Jesus.

No Resurrection, No Hope
Then

No death and no Savior Christ Jesus.

Then our faith would be worthless, yes in vain!

Then no mercy, and no grace given.

Then the Good News message to the world would be a lie.

Then Jesus Christ didn't rise on the third day.

Then no forgiveness for our sins.

Then no hope of Heaven, an eternal resting place,

and eternal Peace

Then no reconciliation with God for our Sins.

Then no need to pray or study the Holy Bible scriptures.

But none of these negative words are true.

For our Savior lives!

Son of the Most High God Christ Jesus

Christ is the reason for any season.

His love is everlasting and endless.

Redeemer for all of us.

Immovable Faith is required to know Him Steadfast, constant, and unmovable in his love for us.

Today, He still brings Hope to the Lost.

Joy awaits you when you meet Him.

Eternal life is his gift to you.

Savior of the whole world.

Unconditional Love He has for all.

Son of the Most High God, He is!

Jesus, I Don't Understand

Jesus, I Don't Understand

How could you love us when we don't do what you ask?

Jesus, I Don't Understand

How did you lay down your life for us knowing we will sin again?

Jesus, I Don't Understand

How did you forgive us when we crucified you on the cross at Calvary?

Jesus, I Don't Understand

Although we don't deserve the things we have already, you continue to love us anyway.

Jesus, I Don't Understand

Even with our despicable, sinful nature, you reach out with your love towards us.

Jesus, I Don't Understand

You love us even with our willfully disobedient nature.

Jesus, I Don't Understand

How you want to be our friend if we only would seek your face?

Jesus, I Don't Understand

How did you love us when we didn't even receive you when you when you came to earth?

Jesus, I Don't Understand

When we forsake you so many times, you still love us.

Jesus, I Don't Understand,

But I am so glad you love and understand us!

My first book's title was "Jesus I don't understand."
My second book's title was
called, "Be a blessing to someone today."

This is my 3rd book, "Divine Blessing from a Sovereign God."

Why Am I Divinely & Truly Blessed?

Because smiling doesn't mean everything in my life is good.

I smile because I have received this blessing.

God's greatest gift is Salvation.

This gift can't be taken away, for it's eternal, like his Love. **Oh, yes, I am truly blessed.**

I have been blessed with a great husband

and a man of God. God gave me great parents,

four siblings, a Godly son and daughter-in-law,

and six beautiful grandchildren.

With all my imperfections, moods, and

temperaments, my family loves me anyway.

Oh, yes, I am truly blessed.

I have the freedom and ability to be a

blessing to someone every day.

My faith helps me to look past my hurts,

my sorrows, and my pains and be thankful for my life.

My Hope is in God's endless love for me forever.

Oh, yes, I am truly blessed.

Many people in my life have passed away but

never your Word God because your love is forever!

I can worship freely and give praise each Sunday to you, Lord. And if I choose,

I can worship you every day!

Oh, yes, I am truly blessed.

How about you? Are you truly & drivingly blessed?

I Will Seek God

When I don't understand, I will seek
God's wisdom for His guidance
When I am tired, I will seek rest in God's loving arms.
When I need a friend, I will seek friendship.
with God's son, Christ Jesus
When I am sad, I will seek gladness and joy in the Lord's presence.
When I am alone, I will seek the closeness
of my Savior, Christ Jesus.
When I need help, I will seek God's Holy Wisdom to guide **me**
When I am unhappy, I will seek joy and delight in God's presence.
When I am grieved, I will seek the Holy
Spirit which God left to comfort me.
When I have a heavy and laden heart, I will seek the peace
of God that pass all understanding.
When I am weary, I will seek my strength in God's Holy Word.
When I am hungry, I will seek the bread of life
contained in God's Holy Word.
When I feel deserted, I will seek God's unchanging
and steadfast love
When I backslide, I will seek the anointing spirit in God's Word.
When I fall by the wayside, I will seek the knowledge
of God to lift me up
When I feel broken-hearted, I will seek God's perfect
joy to wipe away my tears.
When I feel discouraged, I will seek encouragement
through God's Holy Word.
When I need consolation, I will pray to God for His
soothing Words of peace, harmony, and hope I will seek God for
everything I need through Prayer, Praise and Worship!

*"And in the morning, rising a great while before day, he went out, and
departed into a solitary place, and there prayed." (Mark 1:35)*

A Child of God

A child of God surrenders his/her heart and
feelings to the Lord.
When I say, "I am a child of God," I'm not saying that I am perfect.
No, I am saying, I serve a perfect God.
When I say, "I am a child of God,"
I'm not saying I don't have issues in my life.
No, I am saying God is always there to
help me get through any situation.

When I say, "I am a child of God," I'm not saying that I am Holier
than Thou. No, I am saying that my flaws in life are visible to God,
and He still loves me for who I am.

When I say, "I am a child of God," I'm not saying I know everything in
the Bible. No, of course not. I am saying I take time regularly to study
and meditate on his Holy Word.

When I say, "I am a child of God,"
I'm not saying this statement with pride.
No, I am saying that I am humble and sometimes do stumble.

When I say, "I am a child of God," I'm not saying that I am faultless.
No, I am saying my strength, and power comes from the Lord.
When I say, "I am a child of God," I'm not saying that I have all the
answers. No, I am saying that God will lead me,
guide me and walk with me always.

God gives me and you Divine Blessings in His time.

Joyce's Favorite Biblical Scriptures

Psalm 121

I will lift up my eyes unto the hills, from whence cometh my help. My help cometh from the Lord, which made heaven and earth. He will not suffer thy foot to be moved: He that keepeth thee will not slumber. *B*ehold, He that keepeth Israel shall neither slumber nor sleep.

The Lord is thy keeper: the Lord is thy shade upon thy right hand. The sun shall not smite thee by day, nor the moon by night. The Lord shall preserve thee from all evil: He shall preserve thy soul. The Lord shall preserve thy going out and thy coming in from this time forth, and even for evermore.

*****

Psalm 23

*T*he Lord is my shepherd; I shall not want.

He maketh me to lie down in green pastures: He leadeth me beside the still waters.

He restoreth my soul: He leadeth me in the paths of righteousness for his name's sake.

Yea, though I walk through the valley of the shadow of death, I will fear no evil: for thou art with me; thy rod and thy staff they comfort me.

Thou preparest a table before me in the presence of my enemies: thou anointest my head with oil; my cup runneth over. Surely goodness and mercy shall follow me all the days of my life: and I will dwell in the house of the Lord forever.

*****

John 15:7

*I*f ye abide in me, and my words abide in you, ye shall ask what ye will, and it shall be done unto you.

John 15:12

*T*his is my commandment, that ye love one another, as I have loved you.

Jeremiah 29:11–13

*F*or I know the thoughts that I think toward you, saith the Lord, thoughts of peace, and not of evil, to give you an expected end. Then shall ye call upon me, and ye shall go and pray unto me, and I will hearken unto you.

And ye shall seek me, and find me, when ye shall search for me with all your heart.

Proverbs 3:5–6

*T*rust in the Lord with all thine heart; and lean not unto thine own understanding. In all thy ways acknowledge Him, and He shall direct thy paths.

Matthew 6:33

*B*ut seek ye first the kingdom of God, and his righteousness; and all these things shall be added unto you.

Isaiah 40:31

*B*ut they that wait upon the Lord shall renew their strength; they shall mount up with wings as eagles; they shall run, and not be weary; and they shall walk, and not faint.

John 14:6

*J*esus saith unto Him, I am the way, the truth, and the life: no man cometh unto the father, but by Me.

John 15:4–5

*A*bide in Me, and I in you. As the branch cannot bear fruit by itself, unless it abides in the vine, neither can you, unless you abide in Me. I am the vine; you are the branches.

He who abides in Me, and I in Him, He bears much fruit, for without me you can do nothing.

John 3:16

*F*or God so loved the world, that He gave His only begotten Son, that whosoever believeth in Him should not perish, but have everlasting life.

Philippians 4:4

*R*ejoice in the Lord always: and again, I say, Rejoice.

Psalm 34:8

O taste and see that the LORD is good: blessed is the man that trusteth in Him.

Isaiah 40:31

But they that wait upon the LORD shall renew *their* strength; they shall mount up with wings as eagles; they shall run, and not be weary; *and* they shall walk, and not faint.

From my Heart ♥ brothers and sisters to yours

If you are reading this page, God has given you Divine Blessing to be alive this day. I am very humbled and honored that you purchased my book and are on this page of my book. Believe this, we have Hope (Confidence) in our Lord and Savior, the Messiah, Christ Jesus. God loves us and sends His precious son, Christ Jesus to be with us until He returns to earth to take us to our home, Heaven (Paradise).

I'm not a Pastor or a Minister; I am a child of God. I love God's Word and His people which is one of His commandments, to love. And we are all His children, every race, every gender. There are so many religions in our world; Catholics, Hinduism, Agnosticism, Buddhism, Baptist, Muslims, Christianity, Confucianism; and more, but there's only one God! He is the Creator of everything in this world. His beloved son is Jesus Christ. Most of my life, I have studied from the King James Version of the Bible most of the time. In recent years, I have also used the New International Version (NIV for more clarity) to understand the Bible a little better.

My book will only speak of some of the Divine Blessings God has given His people, especially me. I have had many Divine Blessings in my life, but the one I like best is God's gift of Salvation. As a Christian I believe salvation means I was saved from sin and its consequences, which included death and separation from God. We receive our salvation in Christ through repentance and faith. This means turning away from our sinful ways (repentance) and turning to God (faith), trusting in Christ. Jesus will forgive your sins and set you on a path to life with Him. One day I will see God and live in eternity forever. What is a Divine Blessing? To know you are going to Heaven and Paradise and not Hello. Thank Him today!

Another Divine Blessing for me is the gift of my one and only Christian son, Monty Eli Williams. Monty is a very humble and smart young man, a great father, husband, and son. Monty and my daughter-in-law, wife, Lisa, have given me six beautiful grandchildren, three grandsons and three granddaughters, as well as a great grandson. They all know the Lord and His Holy Word. Yes, I am truly Divinely blessed with family. Another one of my Divine Blessings is my longevity from my Lord and Savior. I turned seventy-one years in August 2023. Whew!! Father, I am so grateful and blessed for all those years.

In my lifetime I been able to acquire many wonderful Christian and secular friends. Thank you, Lord.

We all have many Divine Blessings in our life to be thankful for, such as:

- A faithful God and His son Jesus Christ in our lives
- A good marriage or good life being single
- Loving parents, grandparents & siblings
- A lovely home (and we are not homeless)
- A church home to worship at and fellowship on Saturday or Sunday
- To have children, grandchildren, and great grandchildren
- Snuggling on the sofa with your loved one
- A few kind, trustworthy and loving friends
- A random act of kindness from a stranger
- Having Peace & calmness in your life

Trouble Don't Last Forever

Sunrise mornings are unusually cold and dim, with a wind chill; yet our twilight evenings are warmer, brighter, and happier. **Divine Blessing**

When children are crying, shouting, and pushing, yet we find over time they are jovial, calmer, and usually contented. **Divine Blessing**

Uncle Sam always wants 20 percent more of your money than you want to give, yet we are grateful we can pay our taxes. **Divine Blessing**

We see a bad day as an unbearable day, yet we know it's' so much better than a bad life. **Divine Blessing**

We must seek Godly wisdom early in our darkest days, who makes our lives worth living because of his endless love? **Divine Blessing**

Trouble will flee you when you seek Godly wisdom and not human wisdom. **Divine Blessing**

Life's day-to-day activities may seem dim, hopeless, doubtful, and sometimes even uncertain; nevertheless, trouble doesn't last forever! **Divine Blessing**

Thank you, Father. You gave me a Divine Blessing (Jesus)

Your Love was your gift to me, I did nothing to deserve it.

Thank you, Father.

With blind eyes you overlooked my wrongdoings, transgressions, and you showered me with your compassion and new mercies each morning.

Thank you, Father.

You bestow upon me great parents, who gave me so much love and affection.

Thank you, Father.

You allowed me to grow my personal relationship with you each and every day. It can be huge, or it can be very small, it's my choice.

Thank you, Father.

You gave me two loving parents, four siblings, a wonderful son, and a humble husband.

I can never pay you back for these beautiful family relationships.

Thank you, Father.

You gave me your only begotten son, Christ Jesus, to guide me through my life. I will never be the same!

How about you? He loves you too. Thank you, Father.

Admiration
And
Adoration

For God so loved the world, that He gave his only begotten Son, that whosoever believeth in Him should not perish, but have everlasting life. John 3:16

Agape Love

is a selfless and faith filled love.

is a committed and willing love.

is a positive and kind love.

is a patient type of love.

is a boastless love.

is an endless type of love.

I am respectful type love.

is God's nature.

is a noble type of love.

is a sacrificial love.

is God's divine love.

is always in action!

God's Love is fierce.

God's love will divinely bless you when you serve His son,

Christ Jesus.

Freedom and Reflections

For, brethren, ye have been called unto liberty; only use not liberty for an occasion to the flesh, but by love serve one another. For all the law is fulfilled in one word, even in this; Thou shalt love thy neighbor as thyself. Galatians 5:13–14

You Were My Hero; Dad I am divinely blessed to have had a father like you.

I never got the chance to tell you how I appreciated your gentle love and protection that brought me joy.

From you I learned to pray. Your discipline based on love guided by our heavenly father became an example for all your children.

No greater love is shown than God's love for a child who is treasured. Our together times were unforgettable and there are no words to describe those precious moments.

I never heard you ask for much, you gave it all to others.

Your unspoken dreams were silent trying to fulfil my aspirations, hiding your worries from the world.

I hope you knew how much I cared for you, and the strength I found in Your shoulders I cried upon for so many days.

I shout to the world this day, "you were my hero, and so much more!"

Daddy, you made me your princess.

Thank you.

The Characteristics of a Family

Growing, Producing, Changing, and Living are parts of a family,
Sharing, Giving, Loving, and Praying are parts of a family
Personalities, Situations, Failures, and Successes are parts of a family
Misunderstanding than Understanding are parts of a family.

Seasons of ups and downs, good times and bad are parts of a family.
Forgiveness, Tolerance, Compassion, and Longsuffering are parts of
a family Happiness, Joy, Peace, Patience, and Caring are parts of a
family Sowing, Reaping, Depending, and Repenting are parts of a
family Mourning, Rejoicing, Grieving, and Weeping are parts of a
family.

Healing, Recovering, and Rebuilding, Fellowshipping are parts of a
family Love, Grace, Mercy, Blessings, and Favor are what God gives
a Family is not just important, it is Everything! It's God's Divine
Blessing to everyone!

Faith

Faith Lifts the hopeless one to optimism.

Faith Mystifies the atheist who doesn't believe.

Faith Changes the scientist's perceptions of life.

Faith Awakens the teenager's shattered dreams.

Faith Stirs up hope in a new divorcee into renewed hope.

Faith Puts trust inside the unwilling spirit.

Faith Changes a minister's ungodly thoughts to ones of Holiness.

Faith Plants confidence into the unbeliever's mind.

Faith Gives assurance to the doubtful hurting heart.

Faith Excites passion and caring in the unlovable person.

Faith Changes the skeptic's heart and gives it optimism.

Faith Heightens a young couple's love and Expectations.

Faith Lifts the hopeless one to hopefulness.

Faith Takes you from where you are to where you want and should
be in God's will.

Seek Jesus for Peace

Peace is an individual choice.

Do you want Serenity or Chaos? Peace is worth more than wealth, fame, or worldly goods.

Yet people choose not to seek after it. Peace comes in many forms, Serenity, Calmness, Harmony, and Silence.

Yet people choose the opposite feeling, Discord, Uproar, Hostility, and Noise.

Having Genuine Peace makes a bad day bearable, and a good day heavenly.

Seek Peace and you will find true Tranquility!

Divine Wisdom or Holy Wisdom

They are the same thing.
Do you, have it?
Do you want it?
Do you know how to get it?
The Bible said to seek it from the Lord God
Which gives Wisdom, Knowledge, and Joy?
Are these things you seek?
Are you afraid to acquire these virtues?
Is your judgement of people fair?
What do you give back for all you have been given?
Do you labor in vain?
Do you simply eat, drink and be merry?
There is a season for everything.
For life all is vanity and vexation of spirit Seek
Wisdom from Heaven (God) and prolong your life.
Be not wise in your own eyes
Or a fool chasing after the wind
Seek Wisdom and gain understanding!

"The *fear* of the LORD is the beginning of wisdom:
and the knowledge of the holy spirit is understanding.

For by me thy days shall be multiplied, and the years of thy life shall be increased."

Proverbs 9:10–11

Thankfulness
And
Gratitude

In everything give thanks: for this is the will of
God in Christ Jesus concerning you.

(1 Thessalonians 5:18)

So Much to Be Grateful For

You had a child born healthy and normal.
Be grateful
You wake me every morning with my incredible mind intact.
Be grateful
Your elder parents are doing well and are still Living in their own home.
Be grateful
You worked many years on your job, and now you are contently retired.
Be grateful
God gave you your five senses: hearing, smelling, listening, speaking, and seeing.
Be grateful
You have loved and been loved, and now you are in love.
Be grateful
You once were very poor, but now you have prospered.
Be grateful
You once were lost, but now you know your purpose.

Let's be **grateful** for all our obstacles in life; for they have strengthened us through our journey in life.

God will give you Divine Blessings

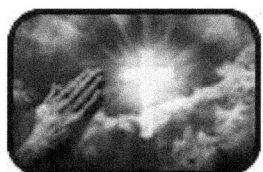

Eased the pain of a broken heart
Stopped the rage of an angry lion in his tracks
Softened the hardened heart of an atheist.
Eased the tears of a mother's pain
Subdued the strength of a raging storm
Quietened the rage of a crowd to a pin drop
Calmed the fury of God's wrath to grace
Healed the war scars of a wounded soldier
Rescued many lost souls to the gift of salvation
Hushed the uprising crowd to a peaceful sound
Remove diseases and sickness back to its beginning
Silence a minister's anger to a goodwill gesture
Soothed a child's tear-filled eyes
Cooler aging sun beams to a beautiful tranquil day
Lightened the load of a tired farmer's workday.
Show forgiveness to the unforgiven
Given mercy to the unmerciful
Show much passion to the undeserving
Provide warmth to a cold heart
Given kindness to you and me
Display compassion to the uncompassionate.
Freely showed charity to an unbeliever

Prayer is the foundation to God's love. Prayer is essential to our
spiritual life as air is to our natural life.

My Morning Prayer

Lord, thank you for waking me up this day,
oh, how I will rejoice! Father, please remove
all doubts in my mind and erase any unclean thoughts,
so, I can be ready to absorb whatever.
You want me to know this day.

Anchor me, Father, right now with your love,
to listen to what you want me to hear this day.
Prepare me to go forth and share what you want
me to share with others this day.

Lord, show me how to empty all my burdens on you,
for you are stronger than I? Remove the clutter in my life so,
I have room for things you want me to bring in.

Father, I know all the good things in my life
comes from you. I am so at awe of your grace
and mercy you give me daily, and I will praise you forevermore
because you care for me. You said to let my requests
be known to you. And, Father, I will.

Teach me to listen with anticipation of your
message for me, as I open my heart so I can hear your
desires for me and my loved ones.

Great is your love toward me, for I am so amazed
you take time to hear my prayer every morning.

Oh, how do you love me? Enrich and empower my walk each
day,
to cheerfully serve you, Lord. Please order my steps,
so, I can be a good soldier in your army.

And I will love one another as you
have commanded of me.

Thank you, Lord, for supplying all my needs
and hearing my prayer this morning!

The Pillars of the Earth
(Trees)

Ancient, majestic, gigantic, and regal in their very stature.
Some with a life span over 500 years or more.
A strong foundation which holds branches and twigs full of
multicolored and one-of-a-kind leaves.

These pillars stand massive, and mighty
with open arms reaching toward the heavens
allowing fowls to glide and land gracefully to rest
and build their nests on branches and
in their hollow trunks.

Mankind's life will never win over these pillars
in the race for longevity on earth.
Their mighty roots descend deep into the earth,
finding unknown places man's eyes will never see.

Their embodied statues have been portrayed
by the old masters on beauty burlap canvasses, to live forever in
museums, cathedrals, and ordinary homes.

These pillars of the earth will be here long after the wars and
man-made destructions are gone.

For they were not created by man but the Creator of man.
They will stand strong until He and only He the
Creator removes them from this world.

Nature Is God's Divine Glory

Look up, look down, look to your left and then
to your right, See the beautiful Heavens and all his Majesty and
know that God's Glory is mystical, endless, and infinite.

The unmeasurable sun testifies to
his glory within the creation of the world.
The Universe is everything above and below that stretches
infinitely into darkness and light; God's Glory
has no boundaries and the Galaxies makes up the Universe
with its stars, planets, gas, dust, and dark matter.

These galaxies are high above the earth.
Hom sapiens have no idea how many galaxies there are
in the solar system Gravity is a force where
everything falls to the center of the Earth.
No matter what you send up
will always fall back down.

It's God's way to let you know,
He is in control of this phenomenal force.
The cosmic vastness my God holds in the palm
of his hand such perspective shifts.
I am small, but I am part of his larger plan.

Earth, the third planet from the sun
harbors life created by God in the very beginning.
The Creator made this planet and everything
in it for his pleasure. The sun is one of
billions of stars that give us light,
warmth, and energy for life.

The Moon is the second brightest object on the side of the sun.
Man has landed on this star, but he couldn't stay
there because of its environment.

The Oceans rules Seas, Seas rules Lakes,
Lakes rules ponds, all part of God's treasures.
The enormous mountains on Earth reach untouchable heights
with their boldness and untouchable peaks.

The Oak tree branches stretches deep
into the soil seeing places no man will ever venture or see.
The Eagle soar over the elevations of the foothills
and rest on high mountain root tops.
The snowy clouds floats across the sky with magnificent
swirls and curls. The waterfalls cascade
downward reaching unknown rivers, seas, and oceans.

The wonders of God's nature will take your breath away.
Our Father uses every possible means to
communicate his Glory to us through Nature.

Be still and know the wonders of our Creator.
He wants to help you find your way home to Him.
Look around today and see God's Glory.

Divine Blessings

D – o good to everyone
I – nspiration or ability to do or feel something creative.
V – ictory with Jesus
I – nspiration or ability to do or feel something creative.
N – ever stop loving Jesus
E – very day is a blessing

B – e a blessing to someone today
L – ove everyone as you have been commanded
E – very good gift come from the Lord
S – how mercy as you are shown mercy
S – tand up for those who can't stand up for themselves
I – nvite others to know the Gospel of Jesus
N – ever look down on anyone
G – ive cheerfully
S – eek ye first the kingdom of God

Thank you for purchasing and reading my book!
God bless you richly.

God's Divine Words

Love the Lord your God with all your heart and
with all your soul, with all your mind and with all your strength.

Love your neighbor as yourself.
There is no commandment greater than these.

Be careful not to practice your righteousness in
front of others to be seen by them.
If you do, you will do, you will have no
reward from your father in heaven.

And when you pray, do not be like the
hypocrites, for they love to pray standing in the
synagogues and on the street corners to be seen by others.
Truly I tell you, they have received their reward in full.

But when you pray, go into your room, close the door,
and pray to your Father, who is unseen.
Then your father, who sees what is done
in secret, will reward you.

For if you forgive other people when they sin against you,
your heavenly father will also forgive you.
But if you do not forgive others their sins, your father
will not forgive your sins.

Seek ye first the kingdom of God.
This promise is made that if we seek it first, and its righteousness,
all earthly wants will be supplied.

Son of the Most High God Christ Jesus

Christ is the reason for any season
His love is everlasting and endless
Redeemer for all of us
Immovable Faith is required to know Him
Steadfast, constant and unmovable in his love for us
Today, He still brings Hope to the Lost

Joy awaits you when you meet Him
Eternal life is his gift to you.
Savior of the whole world
Unconditional Love He has for all
Son of the Most High God, He is!

**Great Prayers
To Know**

The Blessed Beatitudes—Matthew 5:1-10

Blessed are the poor in spirit, for theirs is the
kingdom of heaven.
Blessed are those who mourn, for they will be comforted.
Blessed are the meek, for they will inherit the earth.
Blessed are those who hunger and thirst after righteousness,
for they will be filled.
Blessed are the merciful, for they shall be shown mercy.
Blessed are the pure in heart, for they will see God.
Blessed are the peacemakers, for they will be called the sons of God.
Blessed are those who are persecuted because of righteousness,
for theirs is the kingdom of heaven.

The Lord's Prayer—
Matthew 6:9-13 KJV

Our Father, which art in heaven, hallowed be thy Name.
Thy kingdom comes. Thy will be done in earth, as it is in heaven.
Give us this day our daily bread. And forgive us our trespasses, as
we forgive them that trespass against us. And lead us not into
temptation but deliver us from evil. For thine is the kingdom,
The power, and the glory, for ever and ever. Amen.

The Lord is my Shepherd—Psalm 23 KJV

The LORD is my shepherd; I shall not want.
He maketh me to lie down in green pastures: He leadeth
me beside the still waters.

He restoreth my soul: he leadeth me in the paths of
righteousness for his name's sake.

The LORD is my shepherd; I shall not want.
He maketh me to lie down in green pastures: he
leadeth me Beside the still waters.

He restoreth my soul: He leadeth me in the paths
of righteousness for his name's sake.

Yea, though I walk through the valley of the
shadow of death, I will fear no evil: for thou art with me;
thy rod and thy staff they comfort me.

Thou preparest a table before me in the presence of
mine enemies: thou anointest Yea, though I walk through the valley of
the shadow of death, I will fear no evil: for thou art with me;
thy rod and thy staff they comfort me.

Thou preparest a table before me in the presence
of mine enemies: thou anoints.

But deliver us from evil. For thine is the kingdom,
The power, and the glory, For ever and ever. Amen.

Father, I will continue to run my race until I see you Face-to-Face.

The Ten Commandments

You shall have no other gods before Me.
You shall not make idols.

You shall not take the name of the LORD your God in vain.
Remember the Sabbath day, to keep it holy.

Honor your father and your mother.
You shall not kill.
You shall not commit adultery.

You shall not steal.
You shall not bear false witness against your neighbor.
You shall not covet.

> The greatest commandment:
> You shall love your God with
> all your heart, with all your
> soul, and with all your mind.

The Serenity Prayer
God, grant me the serenity.

to accept the things I cannot change,
the courage to change the things I can,
and the wisdom to know the difference.

Living one day at a time

Enjoy each moment in your life one day at a time.
Appreciate you are so blessed and you
Woke up this morning with your mind functioning.

Understanding we live in a sinful world.
So, we need Jesus in our life to fight our battles,
Who makes things right?

Put your trust in Jesus Christ
And lean not to your own understanding.
Give Jesus the respect He deserves,
Honor, praise and seek his wisdom.

Your life will be so much happier.

Instrument of Your Peace

Lord, make me an instrument of your peace.
Where there is hatred, let me sow love,
Where there is injury, pardon
Where there is doubt, faith,
Where there is despair, hope,
Where there is darkness, light,
Where there is sadness and joy.

O Divine Master, grant that I may not so
much seek to be consoled as to console, not so much to be
understood as to understand, not so much to be loved,
as to love, for it is in giving that we receive,
it is in pardoning that we are pardoned, it is in dying
that we awake to eternal life.

Covenant Prayer – John Wesley

I am no longer my own, but yours.
Put me to what you will, place me with whom you will.
Put me to doing, put me to suffering.
Let me be put to work for you or set aside for you,
Praised for you or criticized for you.
Let me be full, let me be empty.
Let me have all things, let me have nothing.
I freely and fully surrender all things to your glory and service.
And now, O wonderful and holy God,
Creator, Redeemer, and Sustainer,
You are mine, and I am yours.
So be it.
And the covenant which I have made on earth,
Let it also be made in heaven. Amen.

God has Divinely blessed you, what can you do to bless others?

Psalm 121

I lift my eyes to the mountains— where does my help come from?
My help comes from the LORD, the Maker of heaven and earth.
He will not let your foot slip— He who watches over you will not
slumber; indeed, He who watches over Israel will
neither slumber nor sleep.

The LORD watches over you— the LORD is your shade at your right
hand; the sun will not harm you by day, nor the moon by night.

The LORD will keep you from all harm— He will watch over your life;
the LORD will watch over your coming and going both now and
forevermore.

- *The Blessed Beatitudes—Matthew 5:1-10*
- Make a joyful noise to the Lord—Psalm 100 KJV
- The Lord's Prayer—Matthew 6:9-13 KJV
- The Lord is my shepherd—Psalm 23 KJV
- The Ten Commandments—Exodus 20:2-17 KJV

Life is not measured by duration, but by your donation.

- **Mercy Ships.org - $19.00 a month**
- **844-248-1950**

LoveAChild
https://loveachild.com/ways-to-give - 239-210-6107

 **Love is something you do!**

- **Bible League International - 1 866-825-4636**
- https://www.bibleleague.org/
- Give a Bible to those without one!

- **Clean Water**

Life Today. Every well-established provides the opportunity to share the story of Christ and His love, along with lifesaving clean water and its daily supply to children and adults around the world.

'https://my.lifetoday.org/give - 1.800.947.LIFE'

- **Feed The Childrem**

Feed the Children is a leading anti-hunger non-profit organization delivering food and other critical resources to children and families. Our mission is to provide hope and resources for those without life's essentials. 800-6272556

Check out my website to see more things about me.

Joycetreasuresgraves.com (Put in your browser)

Divine Blessings is an uplifting book about the goodness of God. It shares how God blesses his children, Joyce Williams Graves is a true heartfelt Christian and a child of God. She wrote this book, her 3rd, dedicated to the Living God and her love for all His Divine Blessings to her. She is not a pastor, preacher, minister, theologian but she is a child of the Living God. Joyce is someone who simply wanted to thank God for all the Divine Blessings bestowed in her life, and too so many others.

I am not the only one that God gives Divine Blessings too. He gives His Divine Blessings to all believers and followers. God loves everyone! God gave His only begotten son, Christ Jesus to the world. Through His son believers can receive Salvation, a place in paradise and never again be separated from the Father.

Joyce believes divine blessings are God's gifts and favor of His Grace to believers. He sends His goodness to all who chooses to believe. I believe God simply want us to be thankful for his Divine Blessings. I am.

*****

Joyce Williams Graves is a wife, mother, and grandmother, but more importantly she's a Christian, child of God. Joyce started a Bible Ministry, "Project Blessing" in 2016 to purchase Bibles for others to share the "Good News" and bless them all over the world. She and her husband, Glen live in Fort Washington, Maryland with their fourteen-year-old poodle, Energy.

Father, I am so honored to write this book I have dedicated to you. My love for you is very deep and so sincere. I am guided by your Holy Word in the Holy Bible. In scripture, Jeremiah 29:11 kjv, for I know the thoughts that I think toward you, saith the LORD, thoughts of peace, and not of evil, to give you an expected end. God, you plan my life for good, and not harm. You gave us many great promises that you will fulfill. Thank you so much for those promises. Let us rest in God's promises.

God is good to me and you. Thank you, Father.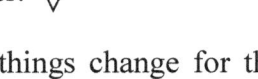

When you know who and whose you are, things change for the better; I will never turn back. I love you father and I thank you for loving me.

joycetreasuresgraves.com

God is all we will ever need.

Jesus is the light of the world.

Holy Spirit is the third person of the Holy Trinity, along with God the Father and God the Son (Jesus Christ).

Remember the promises by God and some of His Commandments.

Promises of God based on scriptures in the Bible.

They are promises for the believer!!

The Promises of God in the Bible Are True. God Is Faithful! You can count on all the promises of the Bible because the God the Promiser is faithful. There are *no broken Bible promises*. They are the sacred word of a faithful God who never breaks His promises. His son Jesus Christ is the living word.

With this new year, we can stand on God's promises. I have two promises that I will stand on and have for many years.

Isaiah 40:31 kjv but they that wait upon the Lord shall renew their strength; they shall mount up with wings as eagles; they shall run, and not be weary; and they shall walk, and not faint. (We want to sworn and our life and have our strength renewed)

Honor your father and mother which is the **first commandment with a promise**, so that it may be well with you, and that you may live long on the earth" (**Ephesians 6:1-3**). Honoring parents is the only command in Scripture that promises long life as a reward.

John 1:9 If we confess our sins, He is faithful and just and will forgive us our sins and purify us from all unrighteousness. (Pastor Duke)

God's promises in the Old Testament **Isaiah 41:10** – God tells us not to worry and promises that He will be with us, strengthen us, support us.

Joshua 1:9 – God commands us to take courage and be strong because He promises to be with us wherever we go.

2 Chronicles 7:14 If my people, who are called by my name, will humble themselves and pray and seek my face and turn from their wicked ways, then I will

John 3:16 For God so loved the world that He gave his one and only Son, that whoever believes in Him shall not perish but have eternal life. (Salvation)

Hebrews 13:5 — NIV Keep your lives free from the love of money and be content with what you have, because God has said, "Never will I leave you; never will I forsake you."

1 John 1:9 If we confess our sins, He is faithful and just and will forgive us our sins and purify us from all unrighteousness.

Isaiah 26:3 "Thou wilt keep Him in perfect peace, whose mind is stayed on thee: because He trusteth in thee.

Matthew 22:37-38 ESV

And He said to Him, "You shall love the Lord your God with all your heart and with all your soul and with all your mind. [38] **This is the great and first commandment.**

Joshua 1:9 – God commands us to take courage and be strong because He promises to be with us wherever we go.

[13] For the promise, that He should be the heir of the world, was not to Abraham, or to his seed, through the law, but through the righteousness of faith. **Romans 4:13 KJV**

Gen. 12: 1,2 I will make of thee a great nation, and I will bless thee, and make thy name great; and thou shalt be a blessing. And I will bless them that bless thee, and curse Him that curseth thee; and in thee shall all families of the earth be blessed. (To Abraham)

James 3:16-17 For where you have envy and selfish ambition, there you find disorder and every evil practice. 17 But the wisdom that comes from heaven is first pure; then peace-loving, considerate, submissive, full of mercy and good fruit, impartial and sincere.

Keep your life free from love of money, and be content with what you have, for He has said, "I will never leave you nor forsake you." **Deuteronomy 31:6 ESV**

1 Corinthians 10:13-18King James Version (KJV) 13 **There hath no temptation taken you, but such as is common to man**: but God is faithful, who will not suffer you to be tempted above that ye are able; but will with the temptation also make a way to escape, that ye may be able to bear it.

Isaiah 26:3 — ASV 3 **Thou wilt keep Him in perfect peace**, whose mind is stayed on thee; because he trusteth in thee

Isaiah 40:31 But they that wait upon the Lord shall renew their strength; they shall mount up with wings as eagles; they shall run, and not be weary; and they shall walk, and not faint.

2 Corinthians 12:9 NKJV
And He said to me, "My grace is sufficient for you, for My strength is made perfect in weakness." Therefore, most gladly I will rather boast in my infirmities, that the power of Christ may rest upon me.

2 Corinthians 12:9 NKJ And He said to me, "My grace is sufficient for you, for My strength is made perfect in weakness." Therefore, most gladly I will rather boast in my infirmities, that the power of Christ may rest upon me.

John 10:27-29, *"My sheep hear my voice, and I know them, and they follow me: And I give unto them eternal life; and they shall never perish, neither shall any man pluck them out of my hand. My Father, which gave them me, is greater than all; and no man is able to pluck them out of my Father's hand."*

Nothing can separate me from God's love.

Romans 8:35-39, *"Who shall separate us from the love of Christ? shall tribulation, or distress, or persecution, or famine, or nakedness, or peril, or sword? As it is written, For thy sake we are killed all the day long; we are accounted as sheep for the slaughter. Nay, in all these things we are more than conquerors through Him that loved us. For I am persuaded, that neither death, nor life, nor angels, nor principalities, nor powers, nor things present, nor things to come, Nor height, nor depth, nor any other creature, shall be able to separate us from the love of God, which is in Christ Jesus our Lord."*

****

Father,

We thank you again for allowing us to come together to learn about your Holy Word. As we begin this new year, let us stand on your promises. Let us trust you and belief in the things you say. Open our hearts, ears, mind and soul to learn of you and your promises tonight. It's a new year, so let us continue to trust, believe, and obey His Holy Word.

Thank you so much, in Jesus Christ name. Amen.

Choose to Forgive and Forget

If someone were to ask you or me to make a list of all the people that hurt you, you and I can probably write out a long list of those who have caused you pain and sorrow, sometimes repeatedly. These may be family members, friends, coworkers, even a friend from church. So many friendships have been shattered because of cruel words and actions that have left those who have been hurt feeling betrayed. You never forget the hurt or the pain someone has caused you. Those feelings run deep. So how does God want us to respond to people who hurt us? Does the Bible instruct us to forgive and forget?

We can turn to the Bible for answers to this question.

The phrase "forgive and forget" is not found in the Bible. However, there are numerous verses commanding us to "forgive one another." Ephesians 4:32 says, "Be kind to one another, tenderhearted, forgiving one another, as God in Christ Jesus forgave you." A Christian who is unwilling to forgive others will find his fellowship with God hindered and impeded and can reap bitterness and resentment.

Luke 6:27-36 also speaks to this issue. In some areas of Christian life, we struggle to find out how God wants us to respond, but that's not the case here. God's instructions are detailed and very clear for us.

Jesus said, "But I tell you who hear me: Love your enemies, do good to those who hate you, bless those who curse you, pray for those who mistreat you" (Luke 6:27-28). In the following verses, Jesus gives several specific examples of how to treat those who have hurt you, and He concludes with, "Be merciful, just as your Father is merciful" (Luke 6:36). He sets the ultimate standard for us.

It's very important that we apply godly wisdom to all relationships we're in. There are times when we will allow ourselves to endure unnecessary pain in relationships because we believe it's our duty or because it brings us to a place of meekness that honors Christ Jesus. While God instructs us to take up our cross and follow Christ Jesus, it's important to discern what God is really telling us through the pain we're experiencing. The closer you become with the Scripture; the more God will speak to you about the relationships you're in. He may be calling you to realign some relationships. You may be around people who negatively influence your life. Painful words and violent tempers can create traps in your life that God may not be calling you to be part of. When you seek God more when it comes to your relationships, you may also begin giving less of yourself to people addicted to gossip and slander because being in that space is not only not uplifting, but also doesn't reflect Christ's spirit.

In these circumstances where you begin to limit the influence of the person that's hurting you, it doesn't mean that you will no longer love, forgive, or pray for that person. It just means that you no longer allow them to take up so much space in your life. We know from Scripture that we are not our own, so regardless of how much we might love someone, including those who have hurt us, we must shift our interaction with them because our Lord tells us to. When we know that we are not our own, we also recognize that things will show up in our lives that are completely outside of our control. God calls us to forgive. As believers, we can choose whether we will hold grudges or practice grace, but if we are truly following Him, the choice has already been made.

This can be tough, so God provides some balance with verses like 2 Corinthians 12:10 which says, "Therefore I am well content with weaknesses, with insults, with distressed, with persecutions, with difficulties for Christ's sake; for when I am weak, then I am strong."

Brothers and sisters, one of the best things we can do for those who hurt us is to pray for them. Many times, and usually, we are not in a place to force the other person to stop their hurtful behavior. We also rarely have the power to change them, but we do have the power to change our response to the person. God simply tells us to pray for them. Yes, pray for them, if you're wondering what you should pray about, the answer is simple. Pray that God will help you to love this person. It's not easy, but it is a commandment of God. Pray that God will help you to see the good things He wants you to do for this person. Pray that God will bless this person and you.

What's so great about these prayers is that they focus your attention on God. Instead of being consumed with the hurt, you focus on God, the One who can heal the hurt, and give you the power to respond in a radically new way. In scripture, King David demonstrates this many times in the Psalms He wrote, speaking of the betrayal of friends and enemies – calling on God to punish them. When David was fleeing for his life because his son Absalom was leading a rebellion, a man named SHimei came out and cursed David and threw stones at Him. When one of David's generals asked permission to take off his head, David responded, leave SHimei alone, perhaps God has told Him to curse me (2 Samuel 16:5-4). This is a powerful response in such a difficult time. David protects Himself from sinning by trusting God and assuming that God's plan is beyond his understanding. Amen.

We can use David as an example in our own lives.

God wants us to trust Him regarding our relationships with others. Ask yourself if the relationships you're in really reflect God. Our best relationships are the ones that have Jesus at the center of them.

It's very possible that if a person is always hurting you, Jesus is not at the center of your relationship with them and that's not healthy for your physical, emotional, mental, or spiritual well-being. If God is not present in the relationship, you're in, it may be time to reevaluate the relationship or at least change the way you interact with each other.

The ideal is to forgive and forget, which isn't always easy to do, I know, but good for our own emotional and spiritual well-being. Remember, love keeps no record of wrongs (1 Corinthian 13:5) and covers a multitude of sins (1 Peter 4:8). Be mindful of those around you who hurt you, and cling to those who love you and have a desire to uplift you. Excellent advice, Lord. Believe in the Lord.

I Won't Complain

I've had some good days
I've had some hills to climb
I've had some weary days
And some sleepless nights
But when I look around
And I think things over
All of my good days
Out-weigh my bad days
I won't complain

Sometimes the clouds are low
I can hardly see the road
I ask a question, Lord
Lord, why so much pain?
But he knows what's best for me
Although my weary eyes
They can't see
So I'll just say thank you Lord
I won't complain

The Lord Has been so good to me
He's been good to me
More than this old world or you could ever be
He's been so good, To me
He dried all of my tears away
Turned my midnights into day
So I'll just say thank you Lord

I want to thank God
He has been so good to me
He's been good to me

More than this old world or you could ever be
He's been so good
He's been so good
He's been so good
So good
So good
To me

He dried all of my tears away
Turned my midnight into day
So, I'll just say thank you Lord,
I won't complain.

Author: Rev. Paul Jones

The concept of divine blessings remains profoundly relevant in today's world. Across cultures and faith traditions, the idea of being divinely blessed holds significant meaning for individuals seeking purpose, hope, and guidance.

Here are a few compelling reasons why the concept of divine blessings continues to resonate in contemporary society:

1. Faith and Hope: For many people, the belief in divine blessings provides a source of faith and hope in the face of life's challenges and uncertainties. It offers a sense of assurance that their lives have purpose and that they are supported by a higher power.

2. Gratitude and Perspective: Recognizing divine blessings encourages individuals to cultivate gratitude and appreciate the positive aspects of their lives, fostering a more positive and hopeful perspective.

3. Spiritual Guidance: The concept of divine blessings serves as a form of spiritual guidance, guiding individuals through difficult decisions, offering comfort during hardships, and prompting self-reflection and personal growth.

4. Connection and Community: The belief in divine blessings often promotes a sense of connection and community among individuals who share similar faith traditions, experiences, and values, offering support and understanding during both joyful and challenging times.

5. Personal Empowerment: For some, the idea of receiving divine blessings empowers individuals to take positive actions and make a meaningful impact in the world, fostering a sense of purpose and a commitment to serving others. Considering these aspects, it is clear that the concept of divine blessings remains relevant and impactful in the lives of many people today, serving as a source of strength, comfort, and inspiration. It is a deeply personal and powerful belief that continues to shape the lives of individuals and communities around the world.

—Media Literary Excellence LLC

But they that wait upon the Lord shall renew their strength; they Shall mount up with wings as eagles; they shall run, and not be weary; and they shall walk, and not faint. Isaiah 40:31 KJV

For God so loved the world, that he gave his only begotten Son, that whosoever believeth in him should not perish but have everlasting life.

https://joycetreasuregraves.com

Joyce William Graves

www.ingramcontent.com/pod-product-compliance
Lightning Source LLC
Chambersburg PA
CBHW051221120626
46547CB00013B/1455